The Last Point

BY ALANA JOSEPHSON

Copyright © 2014 Alana Josephson
All rights reserved.
ISBN: 061559722X
ISBN 13: 9780615597225
Library of Congress Control Number: 2013915619
Alana Josephson
Palm Beach Gardens, FL

This book is dedicated to my family and friends who have all inspired me to tell the truth; there's less to remember.

ACKNOWLEDGMENTS

Special thanks to my mother, without
you this wouldn't be possible.

Special thanks to my sister, Marisa, love you.

Extra special thanks to Leilani, Zoe, Buffy & Willow.

"11 - 10"

I said, trying to smile.

It was hard to do when you have worked your
whole life for this one match –
the finals of
the biggest tournament I have ever played.

Afraid to lose, and happy and excited
about winning - MiXeD emotions.

That was the worst tiebreaker of my life
and here's how it all got started...

The
Last Point

I gathered my balls to serve, put one in
my pocket, and served. It hit the net!
"Oh, great" I said to myself, "just great".

My sister was pacing on the other side
of the glass window, looking at me
like I was in trouble or something.

I pretended to tie my shoe so I could pull
myself together. I took a deep breath.

"Now I have it", I grunted proudly.
I want to do a kick serve, but I don't know how!
That was my only way to win, or so I thought.

So I tried it and my serve soared over the net and into the perfect spot, in the middle of the box.

Suddenly, my opponent called it out! I was so furious! I felt the steam coming out of my ears!

She is a very good tennis player
but she cheats, badly.

Just then, the referee who was watching
our match took us both to the net.
"Start the tiebreaker again".

He instructed us to
start from 0 - 0.
I mumbled under my
breath, "Oh gosh".
I was so tired.

Quickly, it was 11 - 10 on my serve.
The ball went over
the net; she returned it and so did I.
Very hard.

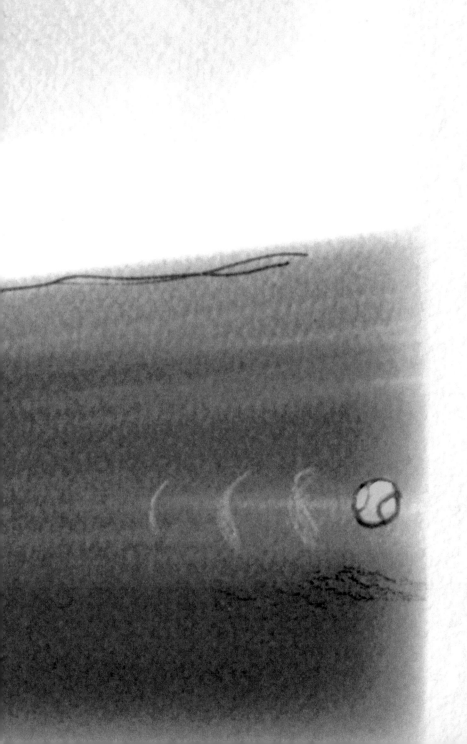

11 - 11 and it's her serve. She hit it hard. I returned it so much harder that I barely saw the ball, even for a split second.

My point!

It was her serve again, and she double faulted! I was about to congratulate myself, to think now I had it won.

But I still had one more point to go. I can do this!

I smashed my return of her serve
so hard; my racquet flew out of my
hand. She missed the shot!

I won!

I was flooded with emotion!

The blood rushed to my head and my knees
felt weak as I collapsed to the ground!

My sister and my mom hugged me
with gigantic smiles on their faces.

We shook hands at the net; then we picked up the balls from the court. I picked up 2 and my opponent picked up 1.

In front of my family and friends, I smiled shyly when they presented me with the winning trophy.

It was a great moment.

I'll always remember what I call,

The Last Point

About the Author

Alana Josephson is a writer who specializes in short stories and poetry based on her real-life experiences. She appreciates how her stories share important ideas like honesty and perseverance in a way that connects with her reader. Her next writing goal is to publish a poetry book for young adults.

Josephson played tennis as a child, winning trophies in her local and regional Little Mo competitions, at the age of nine. She has since retired from competitive tennis in order to pursue her interest in aerial ballet and her blog, DoThisNotThat.com

Made in the USA
San Bernardino, CA
08 February 2019